Going for Gold

Written by Peter Rees
Illustrated by Meredith Thomas

Australia

Contents

Who Is Cathy Freeman?

Cathy Freeman is a great Australian runner. She has won many championships and medals. She has also won many friends with her big smile. Many people admire her courage in speaking out for Aboriginal Australians.

1973	1981	1990	1994
Catherine Astrid Salome Freeman is born in Mackay, Australia.	Eight-year-old Cathy wins her first running race.	Cathy wins her first gold medal and becomes Young Australian of the Year.	Cathy first waves an Aboriginal flag after winning a race.

Setting the Scene

Mackay, Australia

Mackay is a town in northeastern Australia. Its hot climate is good for growing sugar cane. Cathy Freeman was born there in 1973.

Sydney, Australia

Sydney is Australia's largest city. The Olympic Games were held there in 2000.

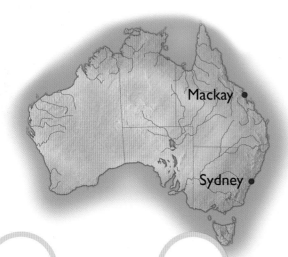

1996	1997	2000	2003
Cathy comes second in the 400-meter race at the Atlanta Olympic Games.	Cathy becomes World Champion in Athens, Greece, and is named Australian of the Year.	Cathy lights the Olympic flame at the Sydney Olympic Games and then wins gold in the 400-meter race.	Cathy retires from running.

Bare Feet

1981

Cathy could run fast. In her bare feet, she was quicker than the other kids, even some who were older than her. Running made her happy. It made her feel as if she could fly. Soon, adults noticed her talent and began to encourage her.

Cathy's family and most of her friends were Aboriginal Australians. Their ancestors were the first Australians. Growing up, Cathy was often treated unfairly because of the color of her skin.

Cathy, age four, and her mother, Cecelia

ancestor a family member who lived long ago

New Shoes

One day, a teacher gave Cathy a pair of running shoes. They were blue and had cleats on the bottom to grip the track. Cathy wore them at the state school championships and won her race. It was her first big win, but it wouldn't be her last!

Cathy's stepfather, Bruce Barber, watched Cathy as she was running. She ran so fast that she made him think of a racehorse. He bought some books about sports and became her first coach.

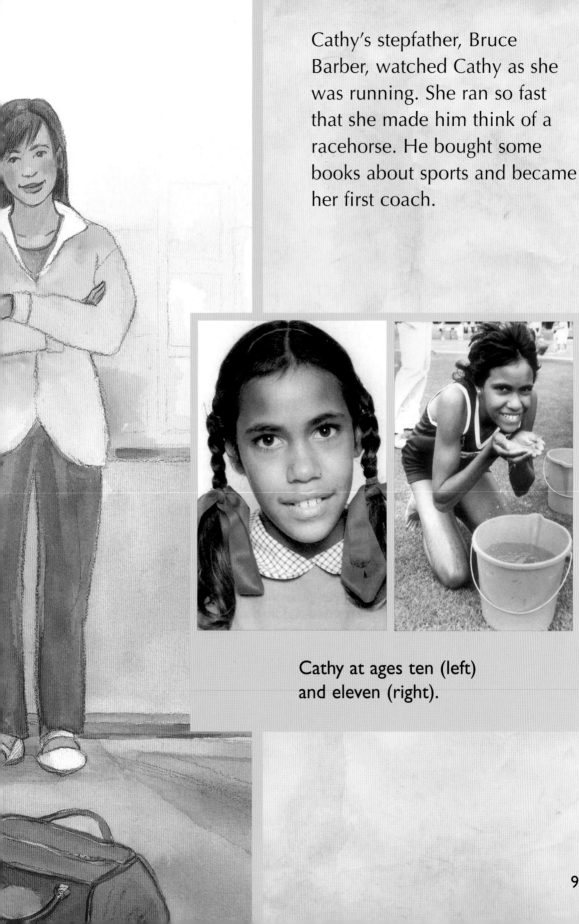

Cathy at ages ten (left) and eleven (right).

Anne-Marie

1988

Cathy wanted to be a champion runner,
but sometimes training seemed too hard.
Then she would think of her sister, Anne-Marie.
Anne-Marie had cerebral palsy. She couldn't run
or even walk. Cathy knew that she was lucky
to be fit and strong. She decided that she
would never give up; she would
run to honor Anne-Marie.

cerebral palsy a medical condition
that causes difficulty
with speech and
movement.

Cathy won a scholarship to a boarding school. There were only two other Aboriginal girls at the school. Cathy felt lonely and homesick, but she was running faster than ever.

At school, Cathy won many trophies and medals.

scholarship money given to a student to help pay for his or her education

A Taste of Gold

When Cathy was sixteen, she was chosen to run for Australia at a big athletic competition in New Zealand. Many of Cathy's heroes from the world of sports were there. It was a dream come true! Even better, she won a gold medal in a relay race.

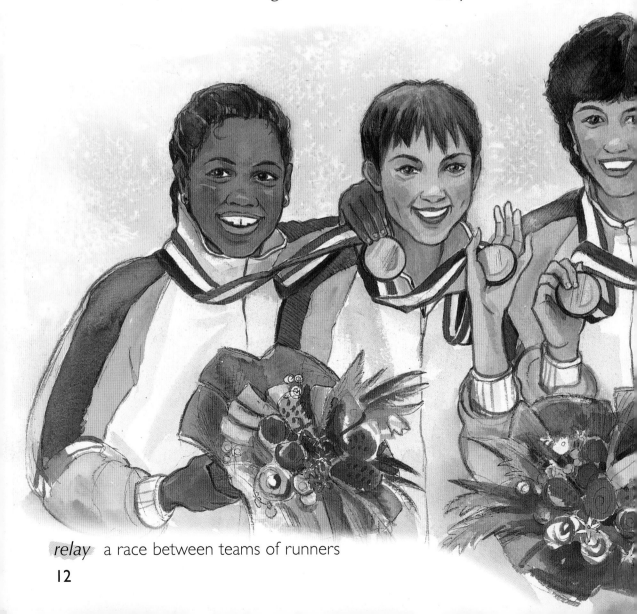

relay a race between teams of runners

Cathy was the first Aboriginal runner to win a gold medal for Australia. Because of her success, she was named the 1990 Young Australian of the Year.

In 1990, Cathy felt on top of the world.

Sadness

On the morning Cathy flew home, she received some terrible news. Anne-Marie had died after an asthma attack. From then on, Cathy vowed to dedicate all her medals to Anne-Marie. However, at the World Championships in Tokyo, Japan, and the Olympic Games in Barcelona, Spain, she lost her races. Everything seemed to be going wrong.

I AM THE WORLD'S GREATEST ATHLETE

Cathy was at a low point in her running career, so she decided to try something new. She wrote these words on a slip of paper: *I am the world's greatest athlete*. She stuck the note on her mirror and read it every day.

Cathy's biggest rival was Marie-José Pérec of France. Pérec (right) won gold medals at the Olympic Games in 1992 and 1996.

The Flag

Slowly, Cathy began winning again. In 1994, she won a big race in Canada. After the race, she waved two flags: an Australian flag and the black, red, and yellow flag of the Australian Aboriginal people. She wanted to show the world that she was proud to be both Australian and Aboriginal.

Cathy grew faster and stronger. She earned the title of World Champion in both 1997 and 1999. She began to plan and train for the Sydney Olympics in 2000. Her goal was to win a gold medal in front of her home crowd.

Aboriginal children celebrate Cathy's gold medal.

Lighting the Flame

The Opening Ceremony of the Olympic Games had begun. All year, everyone had been trying to guess who would light the Olympic flame. At last, a lone figure appeared, holding the Olympic torch high. The stadium went wild with applause. It was Cathy Freeman.

After lighting the Olympic flame, Cathy had to prepare for her races. There were three rounds to run before the 400-meter final. The 400-meter race was Cathy's favorite event.

Cathy ran in pouring rain to win the semifinal of the 400 meters.

400-meter one whole lap of a running track

The Biggest Race

September 25, 2000

On the day of the women's 400-meter final, it seemed like all of Australia was holding its breath. Everybody was glued to the TV as the starter raised his gun. Bang! Cathy was flying. The crowd roared, "Cathy, Cathy!" She made it look easy as she crossed the finish line. Cathy Freeman had won the gold!

Cathy felt dizzy. As she sat down on the track, people with cameras surrounded her. Then she saw her family in the crowd—her mother, her stepfather, and her brothers. They were laughing and crying. She ran over and celebrated with them.

Cathy's family was overjoyed by her success.

Champion

Years ago, Cathy had written her dream on a slip of paper—to be the world's greatest athlete. A dream can become a goal. That day in Sydney, Cathy achieved her goal. However, Cathy's most important goal was perhaps one of her very first: to be the best that she could be. That's a goal that we can all set for ourselves.

Setting Goals

- A goal is a dream that you try to achieve.

- Setting goals helps you plan for things you really want.

- Goals should be exciting, but you may need to set small goals on the way to achieving your big goal.

- If you don't set goals, you will never reach them!

What If?

Cathy Freeman is a role model for young Aboriginal Australians. A role model is someone we look up to and learn from. Role models show us what we can achieve in life.

Name some role models you know about. What if we had no role models? In what ways would our lives be more difficult?

How has Cathy Freeman shown perseverance in her life?

Index

perseverance   not giving up